Original title:
Cosmic Coincidences

Copyright © 2025 Creative Arts Management OÜ
All rights reserved.

Author: Dean Whitmore
ISBN HARDBACK: 978-1-80567-827-4
ISBN PAPERBACK: 978-1-80567-948-6

## Portents from Above

A cat on the roof with a hat,
Chasing stars and a playful bat.
The moon winks back with a laugh,
While planets dance in a cosmic half.

Aliens giggle at odd little signs,
Juggling comets and sipping on wines.
They toss us crumbs from their menus above,
While we keep searching for signs of their love.

### **Destinies on a Celestial Scale**

Two socks disappear in the dryer's spin,
While constellations still know where to begin.
A dance of the stars, a waltz in the space,
As we trip on our feet and forget the pace.

The fridge hums a tune from a galaxy far,
Reminding us of who really drives the car.
Maybe that toast with a heart-shaped burn,
Is a sign that it's time for a cosmic turn.

## The Guiding Light's Play

A streetlight flickers as if to say,
'Not all things here lead you the straight way!'
With shadows that scramble to fit in the lines,
And squirrels with hats plotting humorous designs.

The North Star giggles like it's watching a show,
While the sun applauds with a glowing yellow glow.
As telescopes fumble to catch the right quests,
We laugh at our antics, unsure of the tests.

## **Radiant Revelations**

A shooting star whispers its latest news,
While jellybeans orbit in colorful queues.
The universe chuckles at our tiny strife,
As we flip pancakes and try to find life.

Each fortune cookie laughs at its fate,
With wisecracks that come just a bit too late.
Even the cosmos knows how to jest,
Reminding us all we're just guests at this fest.

## Confluence of Fates

In a café, a cat speaks,
With a hat that squeaks.
A mouse in the booth, oh dear,
Sipping tea, full of cheer.

A dog walks by in a suit,
With a briefcase, who would have thought?
He winks at a squirrel by chance,
And they both start to dance.

Comets crash and collide,
Birds giggle, take a ride.
The moon is wearing blue socks,
As the sun checks his inbox.

Life's quirks line up just right,
In this curious moonlit night.
Jokes written in the stars,
Make us laugh from afar.

## A Serene Constellation

Stars playing peekaboo,
With clouds in a fluffy queue.
A rabbit hops with glee,
As he guides a lost bee.

Planets spin in a whirl,
A wise old owl starts to twirl.
He hoots a tune so bright,
While a comet mimics flight.

Laughter cascades like rain,
Without a hint of any pain.
Galaxies joke and tease,
Turning gravity to ease.

In this quirky ballet,
Time slips and slides away.
Cosmic giggles intertwine,
Creating a grand design.

## **Alignments of the Soul**

Two stars collide in beams,
Laughing hard at their dreams.
A jester jumps with a twist,
In a cosmic comedy list.

A planet trips on its orbit,
With a smile, it can't forfeit.
A comet tells the stars,
'Hold my drink,' before it spars.

Eclipses waltz in pairs,
While time juggles its cares.
The universe plays charades,
In the light of starlit cascades.

With every giggle, things align,
Patterns that simply shine.
In the rhythm of night's scroll,
We find joy in every role.

## Echoes from the Galaxy

A voice from the Milky Way,
Sings to the stars, "Let's play!"
A shooting star recalls a tale,
Of a snail with a comet's trail.

Nebulas spin with flair,
While asteroids start to share.
A dance party on Mars,
With twinkling lights from afar.

Saturn throws confetti rings,
As laughter around it swings.
Space-time stretches in glee,
Where even black holes agree.

Echoing across the void,
Where every quirk is enjoyed.
The universe hums along,
In a never-ending song.

## The Aligning of Dreams

In a world spun wild and bright,
Stars wink at odd sights.
A cat walks in, a dog in tow,
Both chase shadows, stealing the show.

Naps are planned on pillow thrones,
While yogurt spills like ancient stones.
Lemonade dreams dance through the air,
Who knew that daydreams could float with flair?

A waiter drops a tray of beans,
And suddenly life bursts at the seams.
All heads turn, as laughter flies,
Across the evening, beneath the skies.

## **A Dance in the Ether**

Two squirrels plot with nuts in hand,
In their secret, funky band.
They tango on branches, with such flair,
Who knew woodlands had dances to share?

Wind whispers jokes to passing leaves,
While a turtle giggles, as it weaves.
A fish winks at clouds drifting by,
Sharing secrets with a curious sigh.

Lightning bugs flash like disco lights,
As owls chat about odd sights.
In nature's ballroom, laughter's free,
Who knew the night could move like this glee?

## Majestic Constellations

Orion spills his drink on Mars,
While Venus laughs, beneath the stars.
A comet fumbles, trips in space,
And bumps into a smiling face.

Twinkling stars share cosmic snacks,
While craters gossip about the tracks.
Galaxies swirl in a playful spree,
As planets toss space confetti in glee.

A supernova throws a disco ball,
Lighting up the Milky Way hall.
A meteor shower, clumsy ballet,
Who knew the stars could dance and play?

## Celestial Happenings

A moonbeam slips on cosmic stairs,
And giggles echo through the air.
Stardust sprinkles a comet's trail,
As space cats plot their nightly tale.

In galaxies vast, we raise a toast,
To quirky quirks we love the most.
A supernova sneezes, what a sound,
Creating laughter all around.

Quasars boast of light-speed races,
While black holes hide, with puzzled faces.
In the grand circus of the night,
Who knew the universe had such delight?

## Ways of the Universe

Stars spinning round in a waltz so tight,
Planets giggle, lost in the night.
Asteroids bump with a clatter and clink,
While comets sip tea, don't you think?

Jupiter's belly shakes with laughter,
Saturn's rings play the musical master.
Galaxies tease, with a wink and a glance,
While black holes shout, 'Come join the dance!'

A moonbeam slips on a cosmic slip,
An alien laughs, takes a playful trip.
Celestial bodies in a whimsical chase,
The universe sprawls in a playful embrace.

Nebulas bloom like flowers in spring,
Supernovas giggle, what joy they bring!
In the expanse where all quirks align,
The universe chuckles, 'Aren't we divine?'

## **Hidden Miracles of Night**

Night skies shimmer with secrets galore,
The moon throws a party, begging for more.
Shooting stars dive for a tasty snack,
While shadows play hide and seek at the back.

Whispers of wind tickle the trees,
Crickets compose cosmic symphonies.
A dance of the fireflies, twinkling bold,
Each flicker a story of magic untold.

Galactic giggles and sentient light,
Chasing the dreams that soar out of sight.
Bubbles of laughter in the stardust vast,
In the humor of night, our worries are cast.

So lay back, look up, let your heart soar,
The universe laughs, offering more.
With every blink of an eye in the sky,
The hidden miracles wink, oh my!

## Dreaming Under Stars

Whispers of stardust tickle my nose,
As I dream of pizza, in space it glows.
Galaxies giggle, a cosmic delight,
They trade silly jokes, throughout the night.

Planets do waltz, in a swirl of cheer,
With a moonwalking cat, they dance without fear.
Asteroids munch on cosmic candy,
While supernovas blast tunes, oh so dandy.

## Celestial Patterns

Patterns emerge in the quirky night,
A comet with glasses, quite a funny sight.
Constellations argue over who's the best,
While satellites play tag, a cosmic jest.

Stars wear their pajamas, twinkling so bright,
One fell asleep, knocked over the night.
Like a wild dance party, they jive and spin,
The universe chuckles, let the fun begin!

## The Infinite Nebula

In the infinite sea of swirling hues,
Nebulas gossip in glittery shoes.
They trade amusing tales of ancient times,
While cosmic clowns juggle space and rhymes.

Galactic confetti rains on our heads,
As planets spin stories from their cozy beds.
A black hole laughs, with a ticklish squish,
"What's for dinner?" "Just light, with a wish!"

## Rhythms of the Unknown

In the dance of the nebulae, beats go wild,
A starry-eyed comet, a glittery child.
The rhythm is funky, a bop through the void,
With each jazzy twinkle, we can't help but enjoy.

Aliens clap to the celestial sound,
While meteors boogie, spinning round and round.
The universe grooves, in a most playful way,
In the unknown's embrace, let's dance and sway!

## The Silent Symphony of the Spheres.

In the dark of night, the stars all hum,
They jive and wiggle, oh what a fun!
A comet sneezes, bright sparks fly,
The moon giggles softly, oh my, oh my!

Planets waltz in a playful spin,
Each one is dizzy, let the dance begin!
They bump and crash, in a joyful spree,
The darkened void is a grand marquee!

Asteroids chuckle, roll, and glide,
While Saturn's rings swing side to side.
A celestial party, so absurd and bright,
Is this the universe's way to invite?

Jupiter jests with a thunderous roar,
While Venus just laughs and beckons for more.
Galaxies laugh with their twinkling beams,
It's a cosmic caper, or so it seems!

## Stardust Whispers

In the velvet night, wishes take flight,
Whispers of stardust that sparkle so bright.
A shooting star trips, lands with a grin,
"Did you see that? Let the fun begin!"

Tiny meteors play peek-a-boo,
Hiding behind clouds, just me and you.
They shout, "Catch us if you dare!"
As laughter echoes through the cosmic air.

Each twinkle holds a secret in play,
Like cosmic kittens that frolic and sway.
They trade funny jokes in the glittering haze,
While galaxies giggle in a million ways!

So next time you gaze at the sky so wide,
Know that the stars are on joyride.
With every blink, a punchline's told,
In the charming universe, brave and bold!

## Celestial Serendipity

Two stars collide with a wink and a nudge,
Creating new worlds, oh what a grudge!
They giggle and tumble across the vast space,
In a twist of fate, they find their place.

Neptune's kite flies, tangled in clouds,
While Mercury races, lost in the crowds.
A dance of planets, a whimsical sight,
Slipping on starlight, oh what a night!

The universe chuckles, a grand play unfolds,
With galaxies spinning, their stories retold.
Fateful encounters on this stellar spree,
Cosmic pals prancing, so wild and free!

Expect the unexpected, in this void of dreams,
Where whimsy drips down in glittery streams.
Let serendipity lead you this way,
For the best of surprises come out to play!

## Eclipsed Moments

A shadow dances, the sun grins wide,
The earth takes a peek, with nothing to hide.
"Oops, I did it again," the moon starts to tease,
As a solar giggle brings the stars to their knees.

In the thrum of the night, shadows play tricks,
Like cosmic comedians done with their skits.
A moment so bright, then it darts away,
As laughter echoes, gone in a sway.

Rings of Saturn chuckle, "Hurry, come see!"
"We're eclipsing the fun, just you and me!"
As planets all pout and play hide-and-seek,
Making wishes on packages, oh what a peak!

So if you catch light veiled in the dark,
Know it's a joke, and feel free to spark.
In the grand show above, delight is found,
In eclipsed moments, where joy knows no bound!

## **Stars That Speak**

The stars joke softly in the night,
They giggle over our little fights.
While we plan, they twinkle away,
Reminding us of a grand ballet.

A clumsy comet trips on a beam,
As planets laugh, or so it seems.
They whisper secrets to the moon,
And dance along with a silly tune.

Asteroids play hide and seek,
In this universe, absurd and chic.
A dwarf star rolls a cosmic die,
And black holes just wave goodbye.

So when you wish upon a star,
Remember, they're not that far.
They chuckle when we dream and scheme,
In a galactic, glittering dream.

# The Universe Winks

A galaxy winks from afar,
It knows the trouble we are.
Planets spin with a cheeky grin,
While comets race where dreams begin.

A meteor giggles as it zips,
Through the loop of a space-time eclipse.
The Milky Way throws confetti wide,
While asteroids take a goofy ride.

Neutron stars play their game of cards,
While aliens dance in crazy yards.
The universe just loves to tease,
Turning life's woes into cosmic sleaze.

So if you look up with a frown,
Remember, the cosmos wears a crown.
A playful wink could change the day,
In the vastness, let joy have its sway.

## Dance of Destinies

In the dance hall of the sky,
Fate spins and twirls, oh my, oh my!
Stars pair up, do the twist,
In this space where dreams persist.

A rogue planet steps on toes,
While others strike a pose, who knows?
Galaxies join the dizzy tease,
As meteors break out in a freeze.

A supernova busts a move,
In its glow, the stardust grooves.
Time takes a step, then cuts in,
And laughter echoes deep within.

So when you waltz through life's parade,
Think of the dances that are played.
For every bump and silly mess,
There's joy above in the universe.

## Cosmic Echoes

Echoes ringing through the space,
A symphony of a goofy race.
Stars laugh at our earthly plight,
In the depths of the endless night.

Every quasar sings a note,
While black holes hold a sneaky quote.
The cosmos rolls in joyful spins,
With every loss, a giggling wins.

Pulsars tick like a cosmic clock,
Bringing beats that make us rock.
Each ripple dances, sings and plays,
In the universe's quirky ways.

So listen close to the starry tune,
And join the dance beneath the moon.
For in this vast and silly space,
We find our joy and our rightful place.

## Serendipity in the Silhouette of Space

In a galaxy far off, stars did collide,
A pizza delivery lost, cosmic ride.
Aliens craving toppings, oh what a scene,
Ordering pepperoni on a starship machine.

Nebulas giggle, as comets dance 'round,
While space cows moo in a whirl of sound.
Gravity pulls us into laughter's embrace,
In the silhouette of a silly space race.

## Gravity of Serendipity

A meteor shower, and what do you know?
A wish on a pancake, it's quite the show!
Jupiter chuckled, while Saturn spun fast,
As toast drifted upward, a breakfast blast.

Black holes were snickering, while stars took a nap,
In a universe bursting with curious scrap.
Space-time flipped pancakes, oh what a sight,
Where gravity joined in the whimsical fight.

## Cosmic Threads Intertwined

A thread from the Milky Way twirled with a wink,
Stitching up laughs as galaxies link.
Eclipses hummed tunes of outrageous delight,
While quasars danced, twinkling through night.

Starry socks paired with moons on their toes,
Creating a wardrobe of infinity's woes.
And as planets giggled, spinning their yarn,
We knitted the universe with endless charm.

## The Meeting of Milky Ways

Two galaxies met at a cosmic café,
Exchanging their pastries in a playful display.
Supernova frappes shared with a cheer,
While rockets boarded, all clapping in here.

Asteroids juggled planets overhead,
As space-time giggled, no reason for dread.
Connections were made, in a whirl of delight,
In the Milky Ways' meeting, the stars shone so bright.

## Astral Encounters

A cat named Nebula danced in the sky,
Chasing meteor tails, oh my, oh my!
She slipped on a comet, what a sight to see,
Tangled in starlight, a giggling spree.

A squirrel in the galaxy cracked a big nut,
Whispering secrets that left jaws in a rut.
While planets were spinning, they'd throw a grand feast,
With asteroids crashing like confetti released.

Two stars had a meeting, a clumsy affair,
Bumping and bouncing with elegant flair.
They swore they were late for an intergalactic chat,
But really, they just had a date with a cat.

In the end, the moon winked with a grin,
As all the mishaps spun bright from within.
In this universe silly, we laugh and we cheer,
For every misstep, there's always good cheer.

## Fortunate Stars in Orbit

Two stars played poker, with chips made of light,
Betting their orbits through the endless night.
With a wink and a twinkle, they shared their best hand,
While aliens watched, forming a brass band.

A couple of comets crashed into a show,
Trying to dance, oh, how they do glow!
They twirled and they whirled, sending dust in the air,
Leaving cosmic giggles floating everywhere.

A snail on a rocket zoomed past with glee,
Waving at planets, "Come ride out with me!"
But he stalled on a moon, had to take a quick nap,
While the Milky Way laughed at his cosmic mishap.

In this quirky ballet, the stars shone so bright,
As laughter echoed through the velvet night.
Stardust was sprinkled with humor so grand,
For the universe loves a whimsical band.

## The Fabric of Chance

A lone asteroid tried to knit a warm hat,
Wrapped in stardust, he looked quite the brat.
But his yarn got caught in a solar wind swirl,
Spinning and twirling like a cosmic whirl.

A wise old black hole gave him a hand,
Saying, "Let's turn chaos to something quite grand!"
With a stitch of a star and a flash from afar,
They made the first scarf that would go to a star.

The planets all chuckled, "What's happening here?"
As a patchwork of light danced without any fear.
Meteors joined in, in a fashionable way,
Creating a trend that night turned to day.

Out in the cosmos, where wonders all blend,
Every misfortune can be turned to a trend.
So let's laugh at the chaos, embrace every chance,
In the quilt of the cosmos, there's always a dance.

## Echoes of Stardust

In a realm where echoes of laughter reside,
A star named Twinkle felt giggly inside.
She called up her buddies, the mushrooms and moss,
To share in the silly, no matter the cost.

They crafted a joke with a stellar punchline,
That even the planets deemed simply divine.
The sun turned bright yellow, the moon rolled in glee,
While comets looped 'round shouting, "Can you believe?"

One day a supernova threw quite the bash,
Inviting all galaxies, a colorful splash.
With cupcakes of starlight, they danced in delight,
While black holes held secrets and winked through the night.

As laughter transformed into stardust so sweet,
A tapestry woven, where fun and stars meet.
In the cosmos, a joke travels far and wide,
Echoes of laughter that shimmer and glide.

## The Grand Design of Chance

A cat in a hat met a fish on a road,
They both took a stroll, and they lightened the load.
With one silly dance, and a chuckle or two,
They painted the town in a shade of bright blue.

A toast to the moon, that forgot its own name,
It smirked at the stars, calling them all the same.
A wink from a comet, a wink from a shoe,
The universe giggled, as if it all knew.

A speck of green dust on a window so clear,
Joined forces with laughter, spreading joy far and near.
Two socks in a dryer shared secrets and dreams,
Conspired together, or so it all seems.

A squirrel in a bowtie, quite dapper and keen,
Befriends a lost feather, both looking for green.
With jokes about acorns and tales of a pear,
The dance of their fate spun the cosmos in air.

# **Tidal Forces of Fortune**

A jellyfish juggled with a quirky old crab,
They formed a duet, making seaweed drab.
With bubbles and giggles, they spun through the tide,
Inventing new games where no rules could abide.

A bubble below burst, sending fish into fits,
They twirled in a whirl, igniting their wits.
The seagulls all cackled from perches above,
As ocean's own jesters found laughter and love.

A starfish in shades tried to join in their play,
While clams held a concert, they sang all the way.
With a wink and a nudge, they danced on the sand,
The tides laughed so hard, they would take a grand stand.

So next time you wander by water of blue,
Remember the critters who dance just for you.
For fortune is funny, like waves on the shore,
In fits of sweet laughter, we find more and more.

## Majestic Signposts

An owl in a hat waved to a passing bee,
"Chase dreams, little friend, don't just collect free!"
With a flick of its wing and a wink of one eye,
Together they plotted a journey up high.

A cloud's great ambition was sailing with glee,
While raindrops conspired to float like a plea.
With lightning for laughter and thunder for song,
They marked out a path where the weird could belong.

Signs made of hiccups led travelers astray,
Yet fortunes appeared in the quirkiest way.
Each stone on the path, each dip in the breeze,
Had tales of adventures and mysteries to tease.

And so the wise owl took to sharing its cheer,
With the bee fluttering by, always staying near.
Together they'd wander, and sing all day long,
Finding joy in the journey, forever so strong.

## Intergalactic Happenstances

A Martian in shades met a Venusian cat,
With a plop and a giggle, they sat for a chat.
Discussing their planets and who had the best,
They rated their dishes and laughed at the rest.

An asteroid whispered of distant mishaps,
While planets aligned like skilled acrobats.
With nebulae spinning a tale of delight,
They danced through the cosmos, both silly and bright.

A comet named Charlie tripped over a star,
"With a whoops and a whee!" it exclaimed from afar.
While black holes chuckled at jokes lost in time,
They floated their laughter in verses and rhyme.

So if you should stargaze, and find yourself grinning,
Remember those beings, the laughter they're spinning.
For space is a circus of fun and of chance,
In the grand interstellar, we all get to dance.

## **Patterns in the Night**

Stars twinkle in a dance,
Chasing shadows in a trance.
I spilled my drink, oh what a sight,
The cat pounced, ready to bite.

Planets giggle on their way,
While comets tease, they love to play.
A meteor shower—what a catch,
But my umbrella just won't match.

The moon winks with a cheeky grin,
As I trip over a garden bin.
Galaxies roll their eyes so wide,
At my clumsy cosmic slide.

Celestial jokes in every twist,
I laughed till stars began to mist.
In the night, all things align,
Even my socks, well, that's just fine!

## Synchronicity in the Skies

Clouds gather in a perfect line,
Just when I'm out of time.
Rain pours down, but I don't care,
My hat flies off, caught in the air.

Birds chirp a comedic song,
While I dance all night long.
Lightning strikes, a flash and boom,
I guess I'll see you in my room!

Planets clap and share the joke,
While I trip on space debris and choke.
Stars align but I'm out of sorts,
Chasing shadows in my shorts.

The universe is full of cheer,
As I tumble to the atmosphere.
In perfect time, I find my place,
Among the giggling stars, I race!

## The Hidden Hand of Chance

Fate plays tricks beneath the veil,
As I hop on a pesky snail.
A squirrel grins with nuts in hand,
In a circus act that's just too grand.

Crickets chirp a silly tune,
While I'm busy dodging the moon.
Every stumble, every fall,
Makes the universe chuckle small.

A lucky penny turns to gold,
But my mishaps never get old.
A shooting star just missed my head,
While I pondered about my bed.

Cosmic pranks in the endless haze,
Keep me laughing through the maze.
With every twist of fate I find,
A chance to giggle is so kind!

## **Nebulous Harmonics**

The planets sing a silly song,
While I clumsily tag along.
A comet zooms, it shouts with glee,
"Try to catch me if you can, wee!"

Constellations pull a prank,
Decking skies in shades of pink.
I try to dance, trip on my shoe,
As space giggles at my view.

Clouds throw shade, oh, how they tease,
As stars play hopscotch in the breeze.
I laugh until I lose my breath,
With each odd turn of life and death.

Harmonies of the cosmic scale,
Cascade joy in every trail.
In the universe's playful plan,
I'm just a jester, oh man!

# The Rhythm of the Heavens

Stars twirl and dance in glee,
Planets bump, oh what a spree!
Galaxies giggle in their flight,
As comets crash with sheer delight.

A meteor sings a silly song,
While black holes pull right along.
Asteroids play tag in the dark,
While supernovae leave their mark.

The moon winks at the sun so bright,
As they argue who rules the night.
Quasars flash their quirky beams,
All woven into the fabric of dreams.

In this celestial, clumsy chase,
Every flap brings smiles to space.
In the grand dance, oh what a sight,
The heavens keep us laughing all night!

## Celestial Synchrony

Stars align in a bizarre game,
Each one shouts a silly name.
Venus trips over Mars's feet,
While Pluto giggles at the beat.

Saturn boasts with rings so wide,
Yet fumbles when it spins with pride.
Jupiter and Earth share a snack,
While Jupiter tells a cosmic quack.

As meteors zip and zoom around,
They make a sound that's quite profound.
In this quirky, stellar spat,
Even time laughs with a chat!

In this dance of the great unknown,
So much joy from what they've sown.
The universe is a jolly clown,
With laughter echoing all over town!

## Beyond the Veil of Space

Between the stars, secrets lark,
In the dark, they leave a mark.
A portal opens, what a fright!
A cat from Venus steals the night!

As stardust giggles in a swirl,
Planets spin, creating a whirl.
A nebula hums a funny tune,
While a wormhole tries to swoon.

Time winks, but space takes a jest,
Who knew they'd play such a quest?
Each quasar tells a joke so sly,
Laughing with a twinkle in their eye.

In the vastness, there's mischief true,
Galactic giggles are just the cue.
Beyond the veil, fun rules the day,
In this cosmic ballet, come what may!

## Interstellar Fortuity

In the void, odd things collide,
Unexpected friends take a ride.
A comet wears a hat so red,
While stars throw confetti instead.

Planets swap places just for fun,
Daring each other to run and run.
One black hole swirls with flair,
While a giant neutron stares.

Constellations chat in delight,
Painting the sky every night.
And if you listen, you might hear,
Galaxies giggling, spreading cheer.

From every twinkle and burst of light,
A funny tale takes flight.
In this expanse where laughter grows,
Interstellar fun forever flows!

## Universal Threads

In a universe of socks, where pairs go astray,
One always ends up lost at the end of the day.
Stars twinkle in laughter, and planets all cheer,
While our mismatched feet dance in cosmic veneer.

A comet's tail whispers, "Hey, what's your size?"
As galaxies chuckle, spinning broken ties.
Each twirl of the Earth, a quilted delight,
Stitching irony in the fabric of night.

Constellations play games, hide and seek in the sky,
"Catch me if you can!" says the bold shooting guy.
The moon gives a wink, all craters aglow,
While we fumble our dreams, like lost keys in the snow.

In the realm of the bizarre, it's all plain to see,
The universe loves to giggle, just like you and me.
So laugh with the planets, take a chance on the fun,
For in this wild dance, we're all spun into one.

## **Galaxies Aligned**

Two stars crossed paths in a cosmic bazaar,
Each boasting their tales of how bright they are.
One says, "I blazed through a meteor shower!"
The other responds, "Well, I moonwalked for hours!"

At a cosmic café, they sip stardust tea,
Comparing black holes, how dark they can be.
With every mad theory and wild, witty jest,
These celestial beings just want to impress.

Supernova giggles echo through and through,
As spirals of laughter in velvet break through.
Entangled in orbits, with quirks on display,
The universe chuckles while comets sashay.

So next time you ponder the vastness of space,
Remember those stars share a laugh and a chase.
For even in chaos, we find the delight,
In tales of the cosmos, absurdly polite.

## Celestial Convergence

One day Jupiter tripped over Saturn's ring,
Creating a ruckus, the cosmos hiccuped and sing.
Neptune just snorted, while Venus gave cheer,
As black holes rolled over with laughter sincere.

Asteroids giggled, falling out of their lanes,
While meteor showers danced like funky refrains.
The sun made a joke, and the planets roared back,
"Don't quit your day job, you're no comedy hack!"

Galaxies tangled, creating a mess,
With stellar confetti, a shimmering dress.
As stars clinked their glasses in cosmic delight,
Laughter erupted from deep in the night.

So let's raise a toast to this silly parade,
In laughter and joy, the universe laid.
With each twist and turn, life's a playful ballet,
In the grand cosmic joke, we all have a say.

## **Serendipitous Alignments**

A rogue planet tripped on a comet's fine tail,
Spilling some stardust like a cosmic cocktail.
While quasars were dazzled at this goofy show,
Supermassive black holes just giggled, 'Oh no!'

The sun and the moon, in a tango so bright,
Swapped positions and danced through the cool night.
A solar eclipse winked as it played by the rules,
Making shadows that pranced like mischievous fools.

When equinox laughter mingled with glee,
Stars lined up perfectly, just wait and see.
They shared all their secrets through whispers of light,
In the midst of the chaos, everything felt right.

So when stars align and the universe plays,
It's not just the nights or the long sunny days.
In odd little pathways, we find our own groove,
Celebrating the quirks that make life's heart move.

## Illuminated Intersections

In a café on Mars, a barista named Clyde,
Serves espresso to comets that come for a ride.
A planet drops by, in need of a snack,
While meteors dance, and the moon joins the pack.

A cupcake explodes with a sweet solar flare,
And jokes fly around like a light-year affair.
Gravity wobbles as laughter takes hold,
With aliens giggling, oh, how bold!

## The Universe's Canvas

Stars spill their paint on the night's empty page,
Each brush stroke a laugh, each color a sage.
Nebulas chuckle, creating a fuss,
While quarks play hopscotch on particles' bus.

Galaxies twist in a wobbly dance,
As black holes quip, 'We too love romance!'
A canvas of chaos, yet smiled on with glee,
Each splash of starlight, a cosmic marquee.

## Symphonies in Stardust

Asteroids jamming in a rock 'n' roll band,
While Saturn's rings clap, cheering on this stand.
A supernova belting a tune loud and clear,
The universe chuckles, grooving with cheer.

Shooting stars flutter, audition for fame,
As they trip over planets, not one feels the shame.
Melody swirls in the void of the night,
Instruments found in a meteor flight.

## **When Stars Align**

Two shooting stars met in a blink of the eye,
Their paths crisscrossed with a wink and a sigh.
A cosmic blind date beneath soft comet trails,
Laughs echo through space, in whimsical trails.

Umbrellas of stardust, they share and they sway,
As gravity jokes, inviting them to play.
In this dance of the cosmos, silly and bright,
They spin through the galaxies, stars filled with light.

## Each Star's Secret

Stars whisper tales in the night,
Of silly wishes and loves in flight.
They giggle and chuckle, oh what a sight,
While planets spin wildly, full of delight.

Could it be, they play tricks on us?
Or are they just laughing, causing a fuss?
Shooting stars dart, oh what a rush,
As we make our wishes in the cosmic hush.

Look up tonight, give a grin or a wink,
Find the constellations, have yourself a drink.
They're all just friends, don't you think?
Dancing on orbits, faster than a blink.

So next time you gaze at that glittering dome,
Remember each star is not always alone.
With secrets and laughter, far from their home,
They'll tickle your fancy in the cosmic tome.

**When Comets Collide**

Comets are crazy, they zoom and they zoom,
Like kids on a playground, they dance and they boom.
When two meet up, oh, what a groom!
A sparkly wedding in the cosmic gloom.

They create a show with tails all aglow,
Streaking through night, stealing the show.
Gravity giggles, and planets say, 'Whoa!'
As comets collide, a magnificent throw.

The universe laughs, what a time to be bold,
With ice and gas, and stories untold.
Messy encounters, like week-old mold,
But chaos is magic, watch their tales unfold.

So grab some popcorn, it's a stellar affair,
As comets bump into each other up there.
They twirl with a wink, like they just don't care,
In a cosmic ballet beyond compare.

## The Lattice of Lives

In a web woven far beyond sight,
Lives intertwine like stars in the night.
A grappling hook of cosmic delight,
Where penguins and planets have fun in flight.

Fish swim with glee in a gleaming sky,
While squirrels throw nuts at passing by.
A zebra complains, with a sigh and a cry,
'Why am I striped? Oh, how time does fly!'

The lattice of lives keeps knitting the tale,
With jigs and jazz, in a cosmic wail.
Be careful, be kind; don't tip the scale,
For your next-door neighbor could be a whale.

So laugh out loud, let your spirit revive,
In this wacky universe, we all survive.
Together we frolic, thrive and connive,
In this tangled dance, oh, how we jive!

## **Cosmic Cartography**

Sketching the stars with a jovial hand,
Maps of the universe drawn in the sand.
Funky constellations at our command,
Making directions, it's all quite grand.

Find the Big Dipper—you're close, I can tell,
But watch out for aliens, they can yell!
Drawing new paths where the wild things dwell,
In the garden of stars, we giggle and swell.

Orbs shimmer brightly, like gumdrops of fate,
While black holes are just secretive gates.
With a dash of humor, they all congregate,
Laughing at us from a distant state.

So pack up your broom, get on your ride,
Navigate the cosmos, let laughter be your guide.
In this cosmic map, let joy be your stride,
For in the universe, there's nothing to hide.

## Whims of the Universe

A cat on a roof, sees a bird in flight,
Wonders if it's dinner or just a delight.
The moon winks down, as stars play tag,
While Earth stands still, draped in a rag.

A coffee spill, sets off a chain,
The barista shrugs, as the train goes insane.
A love letter lost in an old book's fold,
Only to find, it's worth its weight in gold.

The toaster pops, at the same time too,
Bread flies high, as if it just knew.
A laugh erupts from the kitchen's glow,
As the dog chases crumbs, on an impromptu show.

In the dance of fate, we twirl and spin,
With a wink from chance, let the laughter begin!
Life's quirks and jests, woven tight,
In whimsical chaos, we find delight.

## **Entangled Narratives**

Two socks in a dryer, one goes astray,
Tangled in stories, in a mystical way.
A pencil rolls off, to join the parade,
While the notebook giggles, a memory made.

A bird drops a crumb, right on my hat,
As I ponder the meaning, of this and that.
The neighbor's cat leaps, with surprising grace,
Bumps into my thoughts, claiming its space.

Under the stars, where the oddballs play,
A meeting of minds, in a silly ballet.
The universe chuckles, in its own quirky style,
As time dances on, always worth the while.

In the tales we weave, humor finds room,
With every twist, it bursts into bloom!
Life's strange connections, are no mere chance,
In this odd little world, we all make our dance.

## **Starlit Revelations**

A squirrel in a tree, is an acorn's best friend,
While the lightning bugs gather, to plot and fend.
A comet zips by, with a cheeky grin,
Leaving behind a trail, where the giggles begin.

A paper plane soars, aims for the sun,
Only to crash, with a laugh, not a shun.
The clouds play peek-a-boo, with the bright moon,
While shadows dance softly, to a cosmic tune.

In the night's embrace, dreams start to swirl,
As the universe snickers, watching us twirl.
With each little mishap, joy finds its way,
In the grand scheme of things, we enjoy the play.

So raise a toast, to absurdity's spark,
In this silly existence, let's leave our mark!
With giggles and grins, we embrace our fate,
In starlit revelations, let us celebrate!

## **Threads of Fate**

A missed connection, on a busy street,
Two lives collide, in a wild heartbeat.
A hat flies off, in a gusty breeze,
While a spellbound dog, chases with ease.

In a crowded café, a cup tips over,
Coffee streams flow, like magic, done sober.
A couple laughs, at the unforeseen mess,
Finding love in chaos, who would've guessed?

The sun sips the horizon, as day starts to bend,
While time does a jig, on a whim, my friend.
Each twist and turn, brings a joke anew,
As fate fumbles along, with a quirky view.

So join the parade, with joy in your heart,
For each little blunder, is a cosmic art!
With threads of laughter, we weave the unknown,
In this marvelous tapestry, we are never alone.

## Fate Among the Stars

In the sky, stars collide,
Each twinkle holds a joke inside.
A comet trips, a planet laughs,
While Saturn takes a sip of gas.

Who knew a planet could be shy?
Yet, Venus winks as she floats by.
Uranus giggles, oh what a prank,
As meteors perform, full of flank.

A sunbeam quips in the dark of night,
As shadows dance, without a fright.
The universe plays hide and seek,
In this grand ballet, so unique.

And here we are, beneath this dome,
Chasing starlight, far from home.
With laughter echoing through the void,
Fate's comedy cannot be avoided.

**The Twinkle of Chance**

A shooting star spills a secret wish,
As aliens boil their cosmic fish.
Glazed in giggles, they play their part,
Making mischief from the start.

The moon cracked jokes beneath her glow,
While planets spun, putting on a show.
Mars wore socks that didn't quite match,
As Jupiter plotted a game of catch.

Just around the heavenly bend,
Asteroids bump and then pretend.
They chuckle, twist, and play it cool,
In this vast galaxy, no one's the fool.

With a wink, a wink, and a whoosh of light,
Chance tugs at strings, oh so bright.
In this grand play of the universe wild,
Life laughs along, like a curious child.

## Orbital Encounters

In the dance of spheres, they leap and spin,
Comets and moons wearing a grin.
Stars hold hands and dip with flair,
As asteroids crash, unaware of care.

Galaxies swirl like a cosmic reel,
Each swirl a joke, each twist a peel.
A black hole yawns, devouring light,
Sucking up giggles into the night.

A solar flare gives a cheeky wave,
While gravity says, 'You must misbehave!'
With every orbit, a secret fray,
Stars tip their hats in a humorous way.

Celestial pranks on a grand display,
Tickles the heart in a cosmic ballet.
So let's twirl in starlit jest,
In this universe, we're truly blessed.

## Transient Moments in Time

Tick tock went the cosmic clock,
Planets danced, in a paradox block.
Time trickles down like a curious stream,
In momentary laughter, we gleam.

A supernova bursts with giddy cheer,
While stardust whispers, 'You're welcome here!'
In every heartbeat, in every sigh,
Galaxies chuckle as they pass by.

The clock hands play hide-and-seek,
In this vast vastness, humor's unique.
Eons blend like colors of paint,
A fleeting spirit, a cosmic saint.

So in the vastness where we reside,
Find the giggles, let them abide.
For every moment, fleeting or prime,
Is a chance to dance through transient time.

## Quandaries of the Cosmos

In a vast expanse, a sock went missing,
A black hole swirled, it must be hissing.
Stars giggle softly at our daily plight,
While planets spin tales in the deep of night.

The moon takes selfies, with Earth as a friend,
Mars sends a postcard, saying, "I'll transcend!"
Galaxies dance, in a waltz so bizarre,
But here we are stuck with a question of what's where.

Yet comets bring gifts, like a cosmic surprise,
Wrapped in stardust, beneath twinkling skies.
Oh, the universe winks, with a twist of fate,
While we're just here, pondering our plate.

So we chuckle aloud, at this great charade,
As nebulas whisper, and supernovas fade.
With laughter and wonder, we'll dance through the night,
In the grand jest of the universe, oh what a sight!

## **Astronomy of the Heart**

My heart's a planet, spinning askew,
With asteroids crashing, oh what to do?
Comets with crushes, they zoom right by,
While stars in my eyes make me ponder and sigh.

There's a black hole where my patience was stored,
And meteors crashing, always ignored.
Like constellations, our love forms a map,
Yet sometimes I feel like I'm lost in a gap.

A supernova of laughter, we light up the skies,
While our dreams take flight, like rockets that rise.
My heart sends signals, in Morse of delight,
With satellites spinning, we'll dance through the night.

So let's chart the course of this whimsical spin,
With every odd angle, we'll twist and we'll grin.
Galaxies swirl in this romance so bright,
Forever we orbit, in pure, silly light!

## When Worlds Align

When Jupiter winks, and Venus declares,
A triangle forms, full of quirky affairs.
In the grand cosmic ball, we whirl and we sway,
As comets drop down like confetti on play.

Time bends and stretches, a silly old game,
As each celestial body forgets its own name.
With laughter like stardust, we dodge every rule,
In this universe crazy, we're all just a fool.

Oh, the sun cracks jokes, while the moon rolls its eyes,
In the laugh of the cosmos, we find our own highs.
Starships are born from our silly delight,
Launching us into the comedic night.

So let's toast with stardust, and swing through the haze,
For when worlds align, it's a riotous phase.
Laughter echoes loud in this whimsical space,
In the grand universe dance, we find our true place!

## Enigmatic Orbits

In the dance of the planets, confusion prevails,
Mercury slips through with outrageous tales.
While Saturn just chuckles, its rings all a-blur,
Cuz why wear a suit, when you've got a whir?

Neptune wears glasses, looking so wise,
While Pluto just pouts, 'I'm not small in size!'
Each orbit a riddle, with quirky delight,
A cosmic conundrum spinning through night.

Stars twinkle secrets, their laughter unheard,
As comets crash parties, acting absurd.
With quirky trajectories, we frolic and play,
In the jigsaw of space, we'll find our own way.

So here's to the mysteries, so funny and bright,
As the universe grins in the deep, endless night.
With each little orbit, and each silly twist,
We'll dance through the cosmos, in laughter's sweet mist!

**Unseen Forces at Play**

In a garden, a squirrel did prance,
Trip over a rake – not quite a dance.
The bird on the wire chuckled away,
As gravity seemed to play its own game.

A cat with a hat walked by with a grin,
Stirring up chaos with a mischievous spin.
The clock on the wall said it was time,
For pancakes to fly in a syrupy climb.

A dog wearing goggles chased after a bee,
Barking at seconds as it flew by with glee.
The sun winked down, a bright innocent tease,
As the world spun around with such utmost ease.

And in every moment, the laughter would swell,
As the universe giggled, weaving its spell.
All creatures conspired in delightful dismay,
While unseen forces were hard at their play.

# **Beyond the Veil of Reality**

A goat on a skateboard rolled down a hill,
Spinning out stories that gave laughs a thrill.
The moon slipped on shades, looking quite suave,
As planets discussed how to perfectly rave.

Behind every curtain, a shimmer of fate,
Ducks were debating if humans were late.
A fish in the pond shook its little head,
Said, 'I planned a beach day, but I'm stuck instead!'

Balloons floated high, tied up without care,
While clouds made a pact to play hide and scare.
A jellybean comet winked brightly above,
As odd little beings danced out of pure love.

So in this odd world, let laughter unfold,
With antics and heroes, both silly and bold.
For beyond what we see, the fun is revealed,
In the dance of existence with joy as our shield.

## Starlight Alignments

A toaster once wished on a star shining bright,
Hoping for toast that would dance through the night.
The spoons in the drawer began to conspire,
While forks made a plan to start their own choir.

Stars twinkled down with a wink and a nod,
As a pancake flipped over – the work of a god.
The whisk in the bowl spun stories of old,
While butter and syrup watched legends unfold.

A telescope sighed at the antics below,
As laughter erupted from each cosmic show.
The moon threw a party with confetti of light,
Inviting the sun for the solar delight.

And as galaxies giggled in playful spree,
The universe knows how arranged we can be.
So join in the laughter, take a chance on the fun,
For life's little puzzles are best when they run.

## **Destiny's Hidden Pathways**

A hedgehog in sneakers ran straight for the sun,
Ducking through daisies, it thought it was fun.
The butterflies giggled, playing tag in the air,
While ants set a table for guests unaware.

A wise old owl shouted, 'Hey there, my friend!'
'Watch out for the puddle – it's time to pretend!'
So the hedgehog jumped high, surprise in its eyes,
As destiny chuckled amidst the soft sighs.

A snail wrote a letter, addressed to the stars,
Inviting them over for drinks in the jars.
The moon sent back wishes, each one a delight,
While the hedgehog just grinned at the mess in the light.

Every twist, every turn is part of the game,
As pathways unravel, we giggle the same.
So here's to the journeys – absurd and quite grand,
For life's little whispers are just what we planned.

## Signs in the Celestial Dance

The stars had a party one night,
Venus wore a dress, oh what a sight.
Mars tried to breakdance, but took a spill,
Jupiter laughed, saying, "You're lacking skill!"

Saturn's rings played a jazzy tune,
While comets scooted fast like a cartoon.
Uranus chuckled from behind the veil,
Whispering secrets of an old, funny tale.

The moon lost count of the waltzing pairs,
As shooting stars tried to dodge their flares.
Neptune baked cookies, but forgot the dough,
Yet all had fun in this cosmic show!

So if you gaze at the sky tonight,
Remember the giggles and laughing light.
For in the vastness, laughter prevails,
In the dance of the stars, humor never fails.

## **Harmonies of the Infinite**

A cosmic choir sang out loud,
With quarks and particles in a row, proud.
Neutron danced, a quirky chap,
While photons twirled in a light-speed flap.

Galaxies hummed in a twinkling key,
While black holes whispered, "Hey, look at me!"
Asteroids clapped with rocky hands,
Creating rhythms across the lands.

Gravity tickled the comet's tail,
As orbits circled in a curious trail.
With every note that echoed wide,
The universe laughed, with joy and pride.

So when you hear the universe sing,
Join the chaos and spread your wing.
In this grand tapestry, absurd and vast,
The funny things keep us anchored fast.

## Threads of Destiny Amongst the Stars

A spider spun webs made of light,
Catching wishes under the night.
Each thread connected, a tale untold,
With laughter woven in glittering gold.

While constellations played hide and seek,
Orions' belt snagged a cosmic leak.
Sirius chuckled at the silly fray,
As the Milky Way joined in on the play.

Stars tangled yarns with a wink,
Creating puns that made you think.
With comets swooping in for a chat,
They spun bizarre stories like a cosmic hat.

So look to the skies, don't be shy,
Join in the fun as the night drifts by.
For amidst the stars' delightful spree,
Every twinkle holds a mischievous glee.

## When Planets Aligned

One sunny day, the planets met,
Chitchatting close, without regret.
Mercury quipped, 'I've got the speed!'
While Venus blushed, 'Oh, yes indeed!'

Earth rolled its eyes at a starry tease,
While Mars insisted, 'I do as I please!'
Jupiter winked, a giant joke,
And all erupted in joyful smoke.

The sun beamed bright, casting shadows long,
As they danced together, a planetary song.
Uranus giggled at the tales of old,
While Neptune chuckled, not buying the bold.

So if you find a place to unwind,
Look to the heavens, let your heart be aligned.
In the dance of planets, wild and divine,
You'll discover the humor, pure and fine.

www.ingramcontent.com/pod-product-compliance
Lightning Source LLC
Chambersburg PA
CBHW070748220426
43209CB00083B/120